Two Minutes with God

Damon Welborn

Whitecaps Media
Houston

Whitecaps Media
Houston, Texas
whitecapsmedia.com

Two Minutes with God
© 2014 Damon Welborn

ISBN: 978-0-9883628-7-1

First Edition

Grateful acknowledgment is made for permission to reprint
from the following translations of Scripture:

Scripture quotations marked "ESV" are taken from *The Holy Bible,
English Standard Version*. Copyright © 2000; 2001 by Crossway
Bibles, a division of Good News Publishers. Used by permission.
All rights reserved

Scripture quotations marked "HCSB" are taken from the *Holman
Christian Standard Bible*®. Used by permission. HCSB ©1999,
2000, 2002, 2003, 2009 Holman Bible Publishers. Holman
Christian Standard Bible®, Holman CSB®, and HCSB® are
federally registered trademarks of Holman Bible Publishers

Scripture quotations marked "MSG" are from THE MESSAGE.
Copyright © by Eugene H. Peterson 1993, 1994, 1996, 2000,
2001, 2002. Used by permission of NavPress Publishing Group

Scripture quotations marked "NIV 1984" are taken from the *Holy
Bible, New International Version*®. NIV®. Copyright © 1973, 1978,
1984 by Biblica, Inc. Used by permission of Zondervan. All rights
reserved worldwide

Scripture quotations marked "The Voice" taken from *The Voice*™.
Copyright © 2008 by Ecclesia Bible Society. Used by permission.
All rights reserved

Printed in the United States of America

for the members of Stratford Young Life

Introduction

The idea for this book was born out of a conversation with a junior boy in high school. We were talking about finding time to spend with the Lord. As he went through his schedule, I began to see how he indeed had very little free time. That being said, I challenged him to start with just two minutes a day with the Lord. He could certainly find two minutes. I offered to send him a text each day—a passage of Scripture with two or three questions, and he could take it from there. The questions were usually as simple as, "What does this say about God?" and, "What does this say about you?" or, "What does this mean for you?"

This went on for a couple of weeks before some other kids caught wind of it and they wanted to be added to the list. It seemed that there were many other high school kids whose schedules were jam-packed. There was one girl in particular who began to always ask the question, "What does this mean?" and so I would send her a separate, brief "CliffsNotes" version of what the verse was saying. After a couple of weeks of sending her separate texts, I simply began adding what I would normally send her into the original text.

So for a little over a year now, I have been sending daily texts to these kids, challenging them to spend time with the Lord and learn His character from Scripture. Over time, the title of the texts went from "Two Minutes with God" to a much shorter "2mwG."

This book was created for the typical high school student who has begun a relationship with the Lord and yet is struggling to find time to spend with Him. A relationship, of any kind, will never grow unless you spend time together. The best relationships are forged when you have had enough shared experiences that you begin to know a person so well that you can even know what he is thinking. The great news is God has made Himself known to us in Scripture, and more specifically in the person of Jesus Christ. Now you can know what God is like, learn His tendencies, and find out how He feels about you.

I hope this short book will help get you moving in your relationship with the God of the universe. Surely you can find two minutes in your day. I am confident that if you start with just two minutes a day with God, you will find yourself wanting to make more time to spend with Him.

He is more loving, more powerful, more forgiving, more gracious, kinder, gentler, funnier, and greater than you ever imagined. As someone who has walked with the Lord for almost thirty years now, I can tell you it only gets better the more time you spend with Him. I am so thankful I have taken the time to know the One who made me. My life will never be the same—and I hope you will soon say the same.

Damon Welborn
Houston
May 2014

Day 1

I lift my eyes toward the mountains.
Where will my help come from?
My help comes from the Lord, the
Maker of heaven and earth.
(Psalm 121:1–2, HCSB)

When you first look at the mountains they are spectacular, reaching to the heavens. If you have ever been standing on one, though, it makes you feel small and vulnerable. But when you realize that the power of the One who made the mountains is the same power that watches over you, something even better happens: true peace in the midst of anything. That same psalmist also wrote, "The Lord is for me; I will not be afraid. What can man do to me?" (Psalm 118:6).

The power and majesty of the mountains is undeniable but they are just a mere reflection of the One who made them.

The mountains were made to be enjoyed and explored, but don't forget there is One who is even greater that you can know. When was the last time you enjoyed and explored all He has to offer?

Day 2

Your love, O Eternal One, towers high
    into the heavens.
Even the skies are lower than Your
    faithfulness.
Your justice is like the majestic
    mountains.
Your judgments are as deep as
    the oceans, and yet in Your
    greatness,
You, O Eternal, offer life for every
    person and animal.
Your strong love, O True God, is
    precious.
All people run for shelter under the
    shadow of Your wings.

(Psalm 36:5–7, The Voice)

God's love is as vast as the heavens; His faithfulness reaches beyond the clouds; His righteousness is as solid as mighty mountains; His judgments are as full of wisdom as the oceans are with water. Everywhere you look in creation speaks of God's amazing attributes. And you couldn't exaggerate His attributes if you tried. How do we miss this?! What else in life offers as much as the Creator of it all? It boggles my mind how often I can turn away from this great God, especially given that it never turns out well when I do. I guess you can just claim ignorance, but how long will you continue to *live* in ignorance?

Spend some time to get to know your Creator who offers real life. Instead of looking at the things close to you that can lead you astray, lift your eyes up and see the One who offers you life beyond what is in front of you.

Day 3

When I look at your heavens, the
    work of your fingers,
the moon and the stars, which you
    have set in place,
what is man that you are mindful of
    him,
and the son of man that you care for
    him?

(Psalm 8:3–4, ESV)

It's easy to forget, going through day-to-day life, what is really going on. We are a speck of dust on a giant rock that is just a tiny piece of a giant universe that never ends. When you are able to really put things in the right perspective, you look at life differently, you look at God differently, you look at yourself differently.

It's crazy what we put our trust in for life, given our place in the universe—popularity, money, cars, relationships, even our own knowledge of things. Really? Yet the God who created it all wants to give you real life. It's crazy when you think about it. Perspective is everything in this life.

Go outside today and look around you and think about how you are just one person among billions of people on this earth. Then look up at the clouds and think about how Earth is just one of many planets spinning in the galaxy, which in turn is just one of countless galaxies. Now place all your current struggles and desires in this perspective. Maybe they're not so big after all. Maybe you want to spend more than two minutes a day with God. Just a thought ...

Day 4

Here is a trustworthy saying that deserves full acceptance: Christ Jesus came into the world to save sinners—of whom I am the worst. But for that very reason I was shown mercy so that in me, the worst of sinners, Christ Jesus might display his unlimited patience as an example for those who would believe on him and receive eternal life.

(1 Timothy 1:15–16, NIV 1984)

It seems we are tuned to see things in terms of our worthiness. As soon as we feel unworthy, our confidence sinks. But we are missing it. Paul, who wrote much of the New Testament, calls himself the worst of all sinners.

You see, he realized that it wasn't about how good he could be for God but how good God could be through him. This is the good news of the gospel. God uses us, who are broken and sinful, to show the world His mercy and grace and patience with us. In fact, we spend most of our time trying to fix ourselves, when we should be spending our time spreading the grace and mercy and patience of God to others. This is what you are meant for. I like this translation of the same passage from *The Message*:

"Here's a word you can take to heart and depend on: Jesus Christ came into the world to save sinners. I'm proof—Public Sinner Number One—of someone who could never have made it apart from sheer mercy. And now he shows me off—evidence of his endless patience—to those who are right on the edge of trusting him forever."

Day 5

[God says:] Now look here!
I am creating new heavens and a
    new earth.
The weary and painful past will be as
    if it never happened.
No one will talk or even think about
    it anymore.

(Isaiah 65:17, The Voice)

We live in a broken, fallen world that sometimes feels overwhelming. But don't forget that soon God will make it all new and the things that plague you and make you sad will be no more. Again, life is all about perspective. Having a heavenly perspective makes all the difference in the world.

But wait, there's more! While we long for the ultimate redemption of the entire world we are not just left to wait. We have been given the Spirit who is constantly working and making things new in us. What needs to be redeemed in you?

Spend some time praying and ask God to redeem the broken places in you.

Day 6

So own up to your sins to one another and pray for one another. In the end, you may be healed. Your prayers are powerful when they are rooted in a righteous life.

(James 5:16, The Voice)

There is a danger in keeping personal secrets, one that will destroy you from the inside out. Holding on to your hidden sins will eat away at your soul, cause major damage to parts of your personality, can make you shrink back in relationships, and, most importantly, create problems in your relationship with God. There is something about coming clean to each other and battling in prayer for each other that not only frees us from the power of the secret, but also brings us closer to the One who can heal us and make us whole again.

Finding other believers with whom you can come clean and be real in front of is one of the true joys of the Christian life. It is also vital for finding real peace and healing.

Now, I wouldn't just confess to anyone. Make sure that the other person is a believer and is walking with the Lord, and someone whom you can trust.

Find someone and confess your sins and pray for each other. This is how you walk together in your faith.

Day 7

And let us not grow weary of doing good, for in due season we will reap, if we do not give up. So then, as we have opportunity, let us do good to everyone, and especially to those who are of the household of faith.

(Galatians 6:9–10, ESV)

It is hard when you do things for others and get no thanks in return. It can be just as hard when there are no tangible results for your efforts. So to continue to do good to others, in light of these things, takes relying and trusting in the Lord. We just don't have it in us to persevere in doing good on our own. Remember, though, that life with Christ is not about your ability but in how you learn to trust the Lord for strength.

Find some ways to do good to others today, especially for your fellow believers.

Day 8

[God said,] "Call to me and I will answer you and tell you great and unsearchable things you do not know."

(Jeremiah 33:3, NIV 1984)

Isn't it crazy that the God of the universe answers you when you call to Him? He certainly doesn't have to. He doesn't have to care. But He does. We have a relationship with the Eternal—the One who created the heavens and the earth, perfect in every way, not bound by time or space.

But surely He doesn't know great and unsearchable things that we don't. Not! Of course He does. And you have access to that. We get so bogged down by what we see. Yet if we just turn to Him we are opened up to a world that is beyond what we see. Who can fathom the possibilities?

Call to Him today. Ask Him to open your eyes and show you "great and unsearchable things you do not know."

Day 9

The heavens declare the glory of
  God;
the skies proclaim the work of his
  hands.
 Day after day they pour forth
  speech;
night after night they display
  knowledge.
There is no speech or language
where their voice is not heard.
Their voice goes out into all the
  earth,
their words to the ends of the world.
In the heavens he has pitched a tent
  for the sun …

(Psalm 19:1–4, NIV 1984)

Francis Chan, in his book *Crazy Love*, writes, "Did you know that when you get goose bumps, the hair in your follicles is actually helping you stay warmer by trapping body heat? Or what about the simple fact that plants take in carbon dioxide (which is harmful to us) and produce oxygen (which we need to survive)? I'm sure you knew that, but have you ever marveled at it? And these same poison-swallowing, life-giving plants came from tiny seeds that were placed in the dirt. Some were watered, some weren't; but after a few days they poked through the soil and out into the warm sunlight.

"Whatever God's reasons for such diversity, creativity, and sophistication in the universe, on earth, and in our own bodies, the ultimate point of it all is His glory. God's art speaks of Himself, reflecting who He is and what He is like."

Open your eyes today. Where do you see God? What does what you see say about Him?

God is speaking everywhere in creation. And you don't have to look very far to see it. You are breathing right now without thinking about it, showing how God is giving you life, and your heart is pumping without your control, showing how He is in control. Everywhere He is speaking. You just have to look!

Day 10

For since the creation of the world God's invisible qualities–his eternal power and divine nature–have been clearly seen, being understood from what has been made, so that men are without excuse.

(Romans 1:20, NIV 1984)

God has made a creation that reflects His attributes. Look around you.

"Did you know that a caterpillar has 228 separate and distinct muscles in its head? That's quite a few, for a bug. The average elm tree has approximately 6 million leaves on it. Have you ever thought about how diverse and creative God is? He didn't have to make hundreds of different kinds of bananas, but He did. He didn't have to put 3,000 different species of trees within one square mile in the Amazon jungle, but He did. God didn't have to create so many kinds of laughter. Think about the different sounds of your friends' laughs– wheezes, snorts, silent, loud, obnoxious" (*Crazy Love*, Chan).

Share this with someone else today!

Day 11

[Jesus said] "I have come into the world as light, so that whoever believes in me may not remain in darkness."

(John 12:46, ESV)

Jesus came to expose the things that weigh us down, the things that lead us towards destruction. Much of life can seem confusing and even meaningless, mostly because we live stuck in our sin and many times don't even realize it. We are very crafty and can hide our hurts and secret sins very well from others. The problem is that many times we forget we hid them and they tend to creep up on us unknowingly over time. Unfortunately, when you get really good at this, never really dealing with your problems or facing your sins, you stop feeling and you become numb.

Jesus' light exposes our darkness so as to keep it from destroying us. He wants to bring it out in the open to set you free from it.

Light exposes darkness but also illuminates truth. Jesus' light also brings forth the truth of who we are and what we were made to be. No more confusion or life without meaning. You were made for a purpose!

What is it about you that you are hiding from others or God or maybe even yourself?

Pray and ask the Lord to shine His light in and expose the ugly things, the embarrassing things, and the shameful things that have been hidden. Then allow Him to heal you of that and remove it from you so you can be free of it.

The truth will set you free, but you have to be willing to face the truth first and let Jesus deal with it.

Live free.

Day 12

What matters is not your outer appearance—the styling of your hair, the jewelry you wear, the cut of your clothes—but your inner disposition.

Cultivate inner beauty, the gentle, gracious kind that God delights in.

(1 Peter 3:3–4, MSG)

We spend way too much time on outward appearance. This is not to say you should just walk around unkempt, either. Nor is it saying that jewelry, clothes, or doing your hair is bad. What it *is* saying is that we should spend more time on what is inside. The real you—"that inward lovely light which shines through the window of the human frame" as the author Norman Hillyer put it.

This is cultivating the kind of beauty that doesn't fade. It is an ageless beauty that years cannot wither.

Take this morning, for instance. How much time did you spend picking out your clothes, doing your hair, brushing your teeth, putting makeup on?

How much time did you spend with the Lord working on your inner beauty? You spend all that time getting ready for one day, maybe less than a day. When you take the time to cultivate your inner beauty, that lasts forever. Take the time today—and every day—to cultivate that inner beauty.

Day 13

Be wise in the way you act toward outsiders; make the most of every opportunity. Let your conversation be always full of grace, seasoned with salt, so that you may know how to answer everyone.

(Colossians 4:5–6, NIV 1984)

This is one of the main verses that the founder of Young Life, Jim Rayburn, held dear. The old King James Version says, "Walk in wisdom toward them that are without."

The number one reason people don't become Christians is because of other Christians, mostly because they are hypocritical and judgmental. We are called to be different than that!

As you learn the beauty of the grace that God has for you when you sin (over and over again), this should cause you to be more gracious and respectful toward others.

Another way to look at it is that how you treat others is directly proportionate to your relationship with the Lord. When you have a good grasp on how sinful you are, and how you don't deserve His grace, you tend to treat others with the same dignity and respect and grace that God has shown you—how He has rescued you from the depths.

Your life should reflect the compassion and grace that Jesus had when He walked the earth. He was never dorky about His beliefs and He always showed grace to everyone. He constantly had non-Christians flock to Him because they could tell He genuinely cared.

What would your non-Christian friends say about you? Is your conversation always full of grace? For some of you, your conversation may not be the problem, instead you need to ask if you even *have* any non-Christian friends?

Salt brings spice to things. It also preserves. It enhances. It brings out the best. Is your talk with others seasoned with salt? Does it enhance others? Does it encourage them? Does it bring out the best in others?

Day 14

Don't fall in love with this corrupt world or worship
the things it can offer. Those who love its corrupt ways
don't have the Father's love living within them. All
the things the world can offer to you—the allure of
pleasure, the passion to have things, and the pompous
sense of superiority—do not come from the Father.
These are the rotten fruits of this world. This corrupt
world is already wasting away, as are its selfish desires.
But the person really doing God's will—that person
will never cease to be.

(1 John 2:15–17, The Voice)

A lot of times we obsess about trivial
things. We can spend our lives chasing something that is here today and gone tomorrow.
When we don't get what we want we cry like
a kid at the grocery store when his mommy
doesn't buy him candy. What are you chasing
after right now?

What is keeping you up all night? What
can't you get out of your mind? Is it something
that will last, or is it something that is only
temporary?

Be careful to set your mind on things that
will last, things that matter. There is a battle

for your soul and the enemy would like nothing more than to distract you with things of the world. All of those things seem to satisfy but they never do, do they? You always just want more. We were made to be satisfied by our Creator. Nothing is more satisfying than being in a deep relationship with Him.

Day 15

Don't tear down another person with your words. Instead, keep the peace, and be considerate. Be truly humble toward everyone because there was a time when we, too, were foolish, rebellious, and deceived— we were slaves to sensual cravings and pleasures; and we spent our lives being spiteful, envious, hated by many, and hating one another.

(Titus 3:2, The Voice)

We gain humility when we have an honest estimate of ourselves before God. False humility occurs when we purposely decrease the value of who we are and what we do. Pride happens when we exaggerate the value of who we are and what we can do. Neither is a good thing because they both are an attempt to hide from who we really are.

Once you have a good grip on who you truly are, you are less likely to need to inflate yourself to others. Nor do you have to put yourself down to make yourself look humble. Finding your true identity, which is in Christ, frees you to unapologetically be who you are—no hiding, no masking, no exaggerating the truth. You are infinitely valuable to Christ.

Understanding that changes everything. Anything less than that and you'll be scrambling to compensate.

Day 16

… because there was a time when we, too, were foolish, rebellious, and deceived—we were slaves to sensual cravings and pleasures; and we spent our lives being spiteful, envious, hated by many, and hating one another. But then something happened: God our Savior and His overpowering love and kindness for humankind entered our world; He came to save us.

(Titus 3:3–5, The Voice)

I included part of yesterday's verse because the contrast is startling. It shows what we were: slaves to our own sin—deceived by our own cravings and stuck in a bad situation. "But then something happened…" God, with His "overpowering love and kindness," rescued us from ourselves and the destruction we had heaped upon ourselves. What we had destroyed, God restored. In verse 3 man is the actor, but in verses 4 man is merely the recipient, and God becomes the actor.

I wonder which verse you are living in?

Many people, even though they have a relationship with Christ, still live in verse 3—stuck in shame and guilt and an overwhelming sense that they can't stop a certain perpetual sin. But for those of us in Christ, we live in verses 4 and 5, where the love of God rules and our sins are forgiven and we are free to live without shame and without being mastered by our own cravings.

You are no longer defined by your sin. You are now a child of the living God!

Day 17

… there was a time when we, too, were foolish, rebellious, and deceived—we were slaves to sensual cravings and pleasures; and we spent our lives being spiteful, envious, hated by many, and hating one another. But then something happened: God our Savior and His overpowering love and kindness for humankind entered our world; He came to save us. It's not that we earned it by doing good works or righteous deeds; He came because He is merciful.

(Titus 3:3–5, The Voice)

One of the best parts about being saved from all those things listed in the verses above—and all the death and destruction that come with them—is the fact that we did nothing to earn it or deserve it. If we didn't do anything to earn it, then it's logical that there is nothing we can do to lose it. A lot of people struggle with this; they are afraid that if they sin too much they can lose their salvation. How can you lose something because of "bad works or unrighteousness deeds" if no amount of "good works and righteous deeds" got you there in the first place?!

We have devised some pretty elaborate schemes to feel better about our salvation. Our society has created intricate religious systems with rigid guidelines designed to make us feel better about being a Christian. If we do x and y, we are safe. If we go to church, stop cussing, be nice to people, then we become more deserving of God's mercy and grace. This is so backwards! By definition, you can't *deserve* mercy and grace. Mercy is not getting what you do deserve and grace is getting what you don't deserve.

No, we are saved because He is full of mercy, full of love for us, as these are both aspects of His great grace for us. Stop worrying about all the things you are not doing right and trust that He is working to change you from the inside out. Rest easy and enjoy the free gift God has given us.

Day 18

But then something happened: God our Savior and
His overpowering love and kindness for humankind
entered our world; He came to save us. It's not that we
earned it by doing good works or righteous deeds;
He came because He is merciful. He brought us out of
our old ways of living to a new beginning through the
washing of regeneration …

(Titus 3:4–5, The Voice)

Do you feel stuck? Like no matter what you
do, nothing will ever really change?

This is not the case for those who are in
Jesus. We have been brought out of our old
ways into the new life God has designed for
us. Yet for some reason that old self creeps in
from time to time and you have to remember
that is not who you are anymore.

Forgive the cheesiness of this illustration:

You were like a caterpillar wallowing
around in the dirt, then God transforms you
into a beautiful butterfly. You have the ability
to fly yet you continue wallowing around in
the dirt because that's all you've ever known.
You must learn to get up from the dirt of your
old life. *That's not who you are anymore!* For

those who have trusted in Christ, you have been transformed into something like a beautiful butterfly. It's time to spread your wings, shake off the dirt, and rise above your old life.

And no need to think of yourself as ugly and irredeemable. God has given you a new life and is making something beautiful out of you. This isn't just happy talk—it's what the Word of God says!

Day 19

… He brought us out of our old ways of living to a new beginning through the washing of regeneration; and He made us completely new through the Holy Spirit, who was poured out in abundance through Jesus the Anointed, our Savior. All of this happened so that through His grace we would be accepted into God's covenant family and appointed to be His heirs, full of the hope that comes from knowing you have eternal life.

(Titus 3:5–7, The Voice)

God, through His grace, has given us new life. You are not defined by your sin anymore. You have been accepted into God's family. You are now one of God's children and He is your Father. He is now going to take care of you like a good father should (which a lot of times is thankfully different than how our earthly fathers have done). This is who you are now. You can have hope that you will never have to go back to your old self. You are God's, now and forevermore.

I like this translation of verse 7 from *The Message* as well:

"God's gift has restored our relationship with him and given us back our lives. And there's more life to come—an eternity of life!"

Day 20

For we walk by faith, not by sight.

(2 Corinthians 5:7, HCSB)

It is very easy to get bogged down in everyday life. Life can seem to be too hard and unfair. But for those of us who have Christ, we can cling to the reality that we are connected to Him who loves us perfectly and in whom there is peace. To walk by sight is to let our circumstances rule us. To walk by faith means that we are trusting not in what we see around us but in the One who holds all things together. When we walk by faith, we can rise above our circumstances and live in the peace of knowing Him.

In which are you walking today? By faith or by sight?

Day 21

Who has impeded your progress and kept you from obeying the truth? You were off to such a good start. I know for certain the pressure isn't coming from God. He keeps calling you to the truth. You know what they say, "Just a little yeast causes all the dough to rise," so even the slightest detour from the truth will take you to a destination you do not desire.

(Galatians 5:7–9, The Voice)

At times, you will find yourself in places where God feels distant or where you feel numb or apathetic. I promise you it wasn't because God moved or changed. His love for you is unending and so is His pursuit of you. So what cut in on you? Many times sin is a gradual thing. It starts off with a few "small" compromises and then, before you know it, you're in a place where you ask, "How did I end up here?!"

It's time to return to the One who is faithful. God is longing for you to come back. Remember the truth to which you were called and run back into the arms of the One who will restore you gently.

Day 22

Don't be misled: No one makes a fool of God. What a person plants, he will harvest. The person who plants selfishness, ignoring the needs of others—ignoring God!—harvests a crop of weeds. All he'll have to show for his life is weeds! But the one who plants in response to God, letting God's Spirit do the growth work in him, harvests a crop of real life, eternal life.

(Galatians 6:7–8, MSG)

Here's what the *Life Application Study Bible* says about this verse: "It would certainly be a surprise if you planted corn and pumpkins came up. It's a natural law to reap what we sow. It's true in other areas too. If you gossip about your friends, you will lose their friendship. Every action has results. If you plant to please your own desires, you'll reap a crop of sorrow and evil. If you plant to please God, you'll reap joy and everlasting life. What kind of seeds are you sowing?"

Day 23

Let us not become weary in doing good, for at the proper time we will reap a harvest if we do not give up. Therefore, as we have opportunity, let us do good to all people, especially to those who belong to the family of believers.

(Galatians 6:9–10, NIV 1984)

It is discouraging to continue to do right and not receive a word of thanks or see any tangible results. But what you have to remember, and eventually learn to trust, is that God is in charge of the results and many times we just can't see what He's up to behind the scenes. And we know that if God says you will reap a harvest you can take Him at His word.

When Jesus fed the five thousand there were both believers and unbelievers in that crowd. We should be good to all people. But we also should pay special attention to our fellow brothers and sisters in Christ. Surely you know someone who is struggling in their faith. Even a kind word can go a long way. Prayer can go even further.

Day 24

In him and through faith in him we may approach God
with freedom and confidence.

(Ephesians 3:12, NIV 1984)

It is an awesome privilege to be able to
approach God with freedom and confidence.
Most of us would be apprehensive in the presence of a powerful ruler. But thanks to Christ,
by faith we can enter directly into God's presence through prayer. We know we'll be wel-
comed with open arms because we are God's
children through our union with Christ. Don't
be afraid of God. Talk with Him about everything. He is waiting to hear from you today.

Day 25

But encourage one another daily, as long as it is called Today, so that none of you may be hardened by sin's deceitfulness.

(Hebrews 3:13, NIV 1984)

It can be real easy to wander off into sin which can take you where you don't want to go and leave you places you never wanted to be in. Try and tackle this alone and you're going to get "owned." But there is hope for us in community. That's what this verse is talking about.

Many times it's easier to see someone else falling into sin than it is to notice the same thing about yourself. It's important to find brothers and sisters in Christ who will love you enough to let you know when you are straying. But this has to be done in a loving way and with gentleness and respect.

Make sure you have Christian brothers and sisters with whom you are talking about your mutual faith. Share your struggles and temptations with those you trust. Encourage each other to get up and press on (rather than condemning each other).

The secret to making good decisions and growing in your faith and getting the most out of life lies in community.

Day 26

[Jesus said,] "Blessed are those who hunger and thirst for righteousness, for they shall be satisfied."

(Matthew 5:6, ESV)

When I was in high school I prayed a dangerous prayer. I asked the Lord to give me a hunger and thirst for Him. My life has never been the same. There is nothing sweeter than being satisfied by the One who created you! You might want to pray the same thing.

Day 27

No test or temptation that comes your way is beyond the course of what others have had to face. All you need to remember is that God will never let you down; he'll never let you be pushed past your limit; he'll always be there to help you come through it.

(1 Corinthians 10:13, MSG)

Everyone faces temptations and trials so don't feel singled out. It is a given that you will have these the rest of your life. People who say they'll wait to do this "God thing" till they get older are fools. They certainly have no idea of how good God is and the peace that comes from really knowing Him. Learning to trust God now will serve you well the rest of your life.

Know someone going through a rough time? Share this verse with them. (Or maybe you need to "share" it with yourself!)

Day 28

Be joyful always.

(1 Thessalonians 5:16, NIV 1984)

Make note that this is not saying just put on a happy face. Joy is much deeper. You can manufacture a happy face but joy, joy is not so easy to come by. It can't be manufactured. It is a by-product of knowing and walking with God.

It might help here to understand what joy is and what it is not. Joy is not the same as happiness. Happiness depends on our circumstances and our moods, which in turn have to do with our emotions or place in life. If joy depended on those things we'd all be in trouble, wouldn't we?

Joy is deeper. It comes from the One who is greater than our circumstances, our emotions, and our moods. But so many times we make it about us, our feelings and emotions and circumstances, all of which can change instantly. Real joy comes from the One who holds all things together, and who loves you deeply, and who never changes.

Joy comes from God. It goes past human understanding and circumstances. And *that* is worth finding!

Day 29

… pray continually …

(1 Thessalonians 5:17, NIV 1984)

Don't worry: praying continually doesn't mean you have to kneel for the rest of your life with your hands folded and eyes closed! The more you pray the more you'll find you can pray anytime and anywhere.

This kind of prayer is more of an attitude than an actual uttering of words. It is sort of a centering of self, except you are centering not on yourself but on the One who created you and holds all things together. Praying constantly reminds you that God is in control. We are acknowledging our dependence on Him and realizing His presence in our lives. If you just remember those three things your life will thrive.

Why did God ask us to pray continually? Because prayer is to your soul as breathing is to your body. If you don't breathe, you cannot live. If you don't pray, your soul will cease to thrive.

This is also how you can "be joyful always."

Day 30

Be joyful always; pray continually; give thanks in all circumstances, for this is God's will for you in Christ Jesus.

(1 Thessalonians 5:16–18, NIV 1984)

Don't misread this last part. Paul, who wrote this, is not saying that we should give thanks *for* all circumstances but to give thanks *in* all circumstances. Be careful when you simply say "everything happens for a reason," because not everything that happens to you comes from God. Sometimes things happen in our lives as a result of sin and sometimes things happen because of evil in our world. But when bad things happen we can be thankful for God's constant presence in our lives as well as the fact that regardless of the circumstances we find ourselves in, or why things happen, God is working in all things for our good (Romans 8:28).

Day 31

We are confident that God is able to orchestrate every-thing to work toward something good and beautiful when we love Him and accept His invitation to live according to His plan.

(Romans 8:28, The Voice)

You may think you are not good enough for God or even that you are too evil and self-ish. Guess what? You're right.

On your own you will defile yourself, con-stantly make poor decisions, and probably never really amount to much.

But you're not on your own, are you? No, when you let Christ into your heart an amaz-ing thing happened. Through Him you became righteous in God's sight. He put His Spirit in you to guide you in the right path, the one that is best for you.

And because of that, He is making you into something beautiful and good. Something of great worth. And this is true regardless of whether you realize it. Once you let Him into your life He goes to work. How great it is when you do believe it! To know and believe and therefore rest in the fact that the God of the universe, who loves you, is making you into something great—that's something worth believing!

Day 32

[Jesus said,] "I've told you all this so that trusting me, you will be unshakable and assured, deeply at peace. In this godless world you will continue to experience difficulties. But take heart! I've conquered the world."

(John 16:33, MSG)

This may be one of the coolest verses ever. Why follow Christ? Look around you. Watch the news. We live in a godless world that is falling apart. And things will seem like they are crashing down around you. But while everyone else is freaking out, you can be deeply at peace. Why? Because you are tied to the One who has overcome the world! Learn to trust in the One who can bring you peace in the midst of a world that is crumbling every day.

Day 33

Romans 3:23-24 in three translations:

For all have sinned and fall short of the glory of God, and are justified freely by his grace through the redemption that came by Christ Jesus.

(NIV 1984)

Since we've compiled this long and sorry record as sinners (both us and them) and proved that we are utterly incapable of living the glorious lives God wills for us, God did it for us. Out of sheer generosity he put us in right standing with himself. A pure gift. He got us out of the mess we're in and restored us to where he always wanted us to be. And he did it by means of Jesus Christ.

(The Message)

You see, all have sinned, and all their futile attempts to reach God in His glory fail. Yet they are now saved and set right by His free gift of grace through the redemption available only in Jesus the Anointed.

(The Voice)

This may be the hardest verse to hear and yet coupled with the best news. You have been set free from that seemingly inevitable life!

Day 34

Now that we are set right with God by means of this sacrificial death, the consummate blood sacrifice, there is no longer a question of being at odds with God in any way. If, when we were at our worst, we were put on friendly terms with God by the sacrificial death of his Son, now that we're at our best, just think of how our lives will expand and deepen by means of his resurrection life!

(Romans 5:9–10, MSG)

The power that raised Christ from the dead is the same power that saved you and is available to you in your daily life. If He brought you from death to life when you became a Christian, He can surely bring you back to life from your wanderings. Come back to Him. It's never too late and you are never too far gone.

Day 35

Now it is God who makes both us and you stand firm in Christ. He anointed us, set his seal of ownership on us, and put his Spirit in our hearts as a deposit, guaranteeing what is to come.

(2 Corinthians 1:21–22, NIV 1984)

We, who are prone to wander, are made to stand firm. This is awesome. Imagine if God just said, "I am going to save you and now it's up to you to maintain that." That would be a cruel joke. But He doesn't say that. He says *I will make you stand firm, and I will put my Spirit in you to give you a glimpse of what is to come.* If you have ever experienced a sense of peace, ever had feelings of pure joy like all is right, this is the Spirit in you.

This also tells us that you can't lose your salvation. Once you receive Christ, God has put a seal on us. I get it, though. When we sin and wander off we feel like God has forgotten us or He doesn't love us. But God hasn't moved, we did! Knowing this truth should change everything for you. Turn your heart back to God, His promise still stands.

Day 36

The Word became flesh and made his dwelling among us. We have seen his glory, the glory of the One and Only, who came from the Father, full of grace and truth.

(John 1:14, NIV 1984)

There are times when you feel like God is not there or you are not on His radar or He doesn't like you. This verse goes against all those feelings. God became one of us so we could know Him and be back in relationship with Him. He came with the perfect combination of grace and truth. The best thing about truth is that feelings will come and go, but the truth is always there and never changes. And the best part about grace is that when we react on our feelings, like we can often do, His grace is there to pick us up and bring us back to Him.

Day 37

My guilt has overwhelmed me
like a burden too heavy to bear.
(Psalm 38:4, NIV 1984)

Ever felt like this? You're not alone. Even the great David, described by the Bible as a man after God's own heart (Acts 13:22), felt the devastating effects of sin. So you are not alone in that.

Be careful, though, because there are two kinds of guilt. One that is bad, one that is good. The bad leads us away from God, causing us to hide from Him.

That kind of guilt is not from God.

The other kind, what I am calling the good kind, helps you realize the devastating effects of your sin and leads you back to God. Maybe a better way to say it is there is a healthy kind of guilt and an unhealthy kind.

You have to remember that there is one who is constantly trying to pull you away from God and is very convincing at times making you feel awful about yourself. But also know that there is One who gave up His only Son to bring you back to Him. Don't let the lower-case one win in the battle for your heart. Come back to the One who loves you and has gone to great lengths to make a way back to Him.

Day 38

Summing it all up, friends, I'd say you'll do best by filling your minds and meditating on things true, noble, reputable, authentic, compelling, gracious—the best, not the worst; the beautiful, not the ugly; things to praise, not things to curse.

(Philippians 4:8, MSG)

Our thought life composes a major part of who we really are. Mark Twain wrote, "What a wee little part of a person's life are his acts and his words! His real life is in his head, and is known to none but himself. All day long, the mill of his brain is grinding, and his thoughts, not those other things, are his history."

Now be careful, this is not talking about the power of positive thinking. Because in that philosophy you can lie to yourself, neglecting the hard things you need to deal with.

There is a better source to find what is "true, noble, reputable, authentic, compelling— the best" Do I need to say it? I'll give you a hint, "It is the most quoted Book of all time."

Not the power of positive thinking, but the power of *right* thinking.

Day 39

[Jesus said,] "For even the Son of Man did not come to be served, but to serve, and to give his life as a ransom for many."

(Mark 10:45, NIV 1984)

We spend a lot of time and effort on ourselves—from finding our place in life to getting good grades to finding a good college to getting a good job to getting a great car to getting a girlfriend/boyfriend to being accepted by others to being well-liked and popular to even trying to be a good person or a "good Christian." We can be very selfish people.

Jesus, while He was on the earth, had the potential to have everything for Himself. But He didn't, did He? Jesus chose to serve others. He gave His life away, always sacrificing for others.

You need to know that the Christian life is not about you. It's about giving your life away serving others. Begin today putting your own interests aside and serving others by putting their interests first.

Day 40

[Jesus says,] "Listen! I stand at the door and knock. If anyone hears My voice and opens the door, I will come in to him and have dinner with him, and he with Me."

(Revelation 3:20, HCSB)

Many people think this is written to non-believers but if you read it in context of the whole chapter you will see it is written to Christians who have become complacent and rich.

The pleasures of this world—like popularity, money, security—can be dangerous, causing you to become self-satisfied temporarily. They can make us indifferent to God's offer of lasting satisfaction.

If you find yourself feeling indifferent to church, to God, or to the Bible, you have begun to shut God out of your life.

God is knocking at the door of your heart. He won't force His way in. Open the door up and let the love of God come back into your heart. It's the only way to live life. It's what you were made for!

You might also enjoy

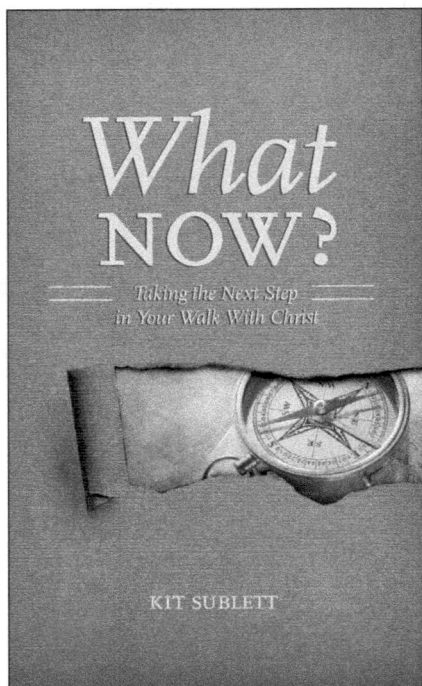

What Now? Taking the Next Step in Your Walk with Christ is great for anyone who wants to jump-start their relationship with Christ.

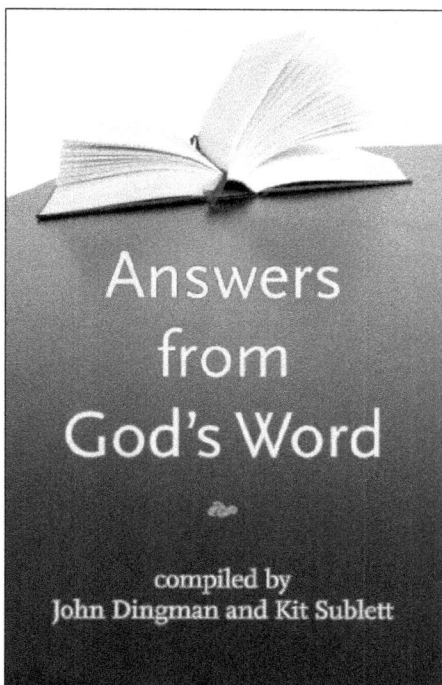

Answers
from
God's Word

compiled by
John Dingman and Kit Sublett

Find out what the Bible has to say about dozens
of topics in *Answers from God's Word*.

These books and other great titles are available at
whitecapsmedia.com or ask for them from your
favorite bookseller!

www.ingramcontent.com/pod-product-compliance
Lightning Source LLC
Chambersburg PA
CBHW062125040426
42337CB00044B/4280